Neath &
Port Talbot

Turn back time

Neath &
Port Talbot
Turn back time

by David Roberts

Courier

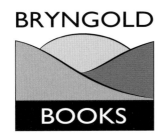

First published in Great Britain in 2005 by
Bryngold Books Ltd.,
Golden Oaks, 98 Brynau Wood, Cimla,
Neath, South Wales, SA11 3YQ.
www.bryngoldbooks.com

Typesetting, layout and design
by Bryngold Books

ISBN 0-9547859-5-9

Printed in Wales by
Dinefwr Press, Rawlings Road,
Llandybie, Carmarthenshire, SA18 3YD

Contents

An appreciation

Neath & Port Talbot Turn Back Time would not have been made possible without the valued assistance of readers of the South Wales Evening Post and Courier readers together with the many residents of both towns, past and present, who so willingly submitted their own cherished personal images of days gone by. However small their contribution it is just as valuable in making this a book that is by the people, for the people.

Particular thanks are due to:

Cheryl Roberts,
Roger & Veronica Gale, Keith and Anne Davies,
John Newman, Peter Sodestrom, Bill Young,
Jeff Thomas, Brian Arnold,
John Vivian Hughes, Annette Jones,
Neath Port Talbot Libraries and Museum service,
Audrey Walters, Steve Dinham, Peter Stephens,
Glenys Landeg, Gerrard Lewis, Denys Parsons,
John Howells, Anita Care, Gillian Evans,
Jenny Lewis, Graham Isaac, J. T. Hughes,
David Richards, Val & Mike Davies,
Graham & Diane Gilbert, Miss Pope,
Norman & Winifred Reed, Arthur Croft,
Anne George, Mrs D Morris, Mary Roberts,
Mark & Margaret Lemon, Betty Haines,
Anita Thomas, Colin & Jean Griffiths, Mr & Mrs Barnes,
Bethan Healey, Alan Saunders, Dennis Rees, Phyllis Meaton,
Phillip Curnow, Adrian Hughes, Betty Hall
John Southard, Colin Scott, Huw Evans and Anthony Isaac,
Airphotos Archive, Also Emyr Nicholas and
staff at Dinefwr Press for their support.

For details of how you can contribute to the next book and in doing so play a part in this valuable, growing pictorial archive telephone 01639 643961. All contributions for the next publication will be welcomed and returned after use. All photographic formats are acceptable.

Foreword

THE publication of Neath and Port Talbot Turn Back Time is a further remarkable achievement by David Roberts.

The number of photographs diligently gathered and published by David since he began his series of books must now number several thousand.

Those books have captured for this and future generations a social map of the world inhabited by our forefathers. A world in which, while some things have remained reassuringly similar, far more has changed out of all recognition.

Faces and places in these pages speak to us of occupations, events and pastimes that have slipped into history while we have been busy getting on with our modern lives.

The memories they stir leave us once again in David's debt for the sheer hard work he has put in to gather another collection of fascinating images. Well done, to him.

Spencer Feeney,
Editor,
South Wales Evening Post

Two towns with one heart

Neath and Port Talbot are two, long-established, neighbouring towns that are very similar in outlook and yet at the same time can be observed to be markedly different. They have shared the growing pains experienced as the days of agriculture melted under the heat of the industrial revolution and they have both stood brave in the face of enormous redundancies thrust upon them as traditional, heavy industries such as iron, steel and coal contracted.

Today the County Borough of Neath Port Talbot flies its flag proud and high in a bid to attract fresh hi-tech employment providing opportunities in tune with the 21st Century and, when it is successful, both towns benefit.

Yet closer examination will reveal many ways in which time has allowed them to retain many differences. Compare their town centres for example and it is easy to observe that while Port Talbot succumbed to almost total redevelopment, Neath has retained its Victorian appeal. Each of course has its own attraction to local residents and visitors alike. Scratch the surface and further differences are quickly revealed. In particular their own distinct traditions, some of which are reflected within these pages.

It is this that makes any peep back at the past of the two towns that today share one heart, and the communities within them compellingly interesting. It is this too that makes the seventh in this series of pictorial nostalgia books to appear in consecutive years just as fresh and as fascinating as the first.

David Roberts,
2005.

Street life

Windsor Road, looking towards Stockham's Corner from Holloway's Corner, early 1900s. The houses at the centre of this scene show that Neath Methodist Chapel — the Penny Brick Chapel — had yet to be built.

Water Street, Aberavon, early 1900s. This was the view looking up towards its junction with High Street. Both vanished under town centre redevelopment during the early 1970s.

A group of Neath youngsters gather on land that later became the town's Victoria Gardens, 1895. Were they on their way home from Alderman Davies' School in the background perhaps?

Looking across Aberavon from Mynydd Dinas, 1910.

The bridge over the River Afan at High Street, Aberavon, 1900. The Walnut Tree Hotel is just visible on the right.

This was the former YWCA building that stood in London Road, Neath, seen around 1910

Pentyla, Port Talbot, looking towards Baglan, 1910.

Looking up lower Water Street, Aberavon, 1910.

Some of the staff and customers pose for the photographer outside the The Post Office at Eastland Road, Neath, early 1900s.

The Square, Neath, early 1920s.

Looking up Station Road, Port Talbot, towards the centre of the town, 1915.

The County School Neath, later Neath Girls Grammar School, on Cadoxton Road, late 1920s

An interesting view of Victoria Square, Aberavon, in the early 1920s.

A fascinating aerial view of Aberavon, 1929.

Victoria Gardens, Neath, 1924.

The interior of Gnoll Congregational Church, Library Road, Neath, mid-1930s.

A policeman on traffic point duty at the junction of Water Street and High Street, Aberavon, at one time the worst traffic bottleneck in Wales, late 1930s.

One for the album! A family pose for a picture with Margam Terrace, Port Talbot, behind them, early 1950s.

High Street, Aberavon, looking westwards towards Pentyla, late 1950s.

Wellfield Avenue, Neath, early 1950s, with one of its young inhabitants.

Wind Street, Neath, showing the Boots the Chemist store, 1957. It later moved to new premises in Green Street before relocating yet again to its larger, current site at the junction of Wind Street and Water Street.

Some of the stores that traded in Water Street, Aberavon, in 1967 before town centre redevelopment. The Walnut Tree Hotel is on the left and the public hall above shops in the centre of this view towards High Street.

The Christmas tree in Victoria Gardens, 1964.

The impressive frontage of Aberavon Workingmen's Club, Talbot Square, 1967.

Angel Hotel, High Street, Aberavon, 1967. Alongside are the premises of N. Campisi, a popular local tailor.

Buildings at the end of Old Market Street, Neath, 1965.

A late 1960s view across the rooftops of a long vanished part of Aberavon. The Castle Hotel in the foreground was in Water Street.

The lodge on Cimla Road, Neath, leading to the Gnoll Grounds entrance. It was demolished shortly after this picture was taken in 1966 and later replaced by a detached house.

Construction of Neath Civic Centre, Prince of Wales Drive, 1962. The foundation stone was laid on September 17, 1962. The building consisted of two wings. One was occupied by Neath Rural District Council in 1964 and the other by Neath Borough Council in 1965. It was officially opened a year later.

The Maypole grocery store and Walnut Tree Hotel, at the junction of Water Street and High Street, Port Talbot about 1970. The David Evans store is also tucked away on the left.

Neath's low level Riverside railway station, Bridge Street, 1966. It originally served the Neath & Brecon Railway.

Looking westwards along High Street, Aberavon, with the Globe Hotel prominent, late 1960s.

Much of the centre of old Aberavon had been demolished to make way for town centre redevelopment by the time this picture was taken in 1972.

Cattle Street, Neath, showing the Corn Stores, 1966 and looking from Angel Street in the direction of the castle.

This was the entrance to the former National Board School, Queen Street, Neath. The building was used by the Guardian newspaper until this picture was taken when it moved to new premises in nearby London Road in 1967.

The raised section of the M4 motorway across Port Talbot at an advanced stage of construction in 1964. The completed motorway channelled through traffic away from the centre of the town and eased one of the worst traffic bottlenecks in Wales.

Orchard Street, Neath, October 1966. A wide, red band had been painted on all the buildings taken over by Woolworths for its store enlargement programme.

Looking towards Bridge Street, Neath, from the junction of The Croft and Angel Street, April 1967.

This area was formerly High Street, Aberavon. It is seen after demolition of the last of its properties and during construction of the Aberafan Centre, 1975.

Looking along the M4 towards Port Talbot with the town's steelworks in the background, late-1970s.

Ena Avenue, Neath, after it had snowed, December 1967.

The junction of Station Road and Bethany Square, Port Talbot, early 1980s.

The scene after demolition of properties in Queen Street, Neath had cleared the way for the building of the town's first Tesco supermarket. Now the site is occupied by a Hyper Value store, 1968.

Neath's former town hall, Church Place,1969 with Matthews Decolympia store in the background in New Street.

Talcennau Road, Port Talbot, looking seawards, after heavy snowfall, early 1982.

Neath's southern link road under construction onto Windsor Road, 1969.

Sandfields Road, Aberavon, mid-1980s.

The site of Neath Port Talbot County Borough Council's civic centre in 1985 — just a car park.

Water Street, Neath, looking towards the Cross Keys pub, 1972.

Looking eastwards along Station Road, Port Talbot, 1986.

Originally the Congregational Chapel, Cwmavon Road, Port Talbot and later the 'Belt and Bayonet Club', this building was derelict and overshadowed by the M4 motorway, when this mid-1980s scene was captured.

Looking up Angel Street towards The Square, Neath 1972.

Station Road, Port Talbot, resplendent with its Christmas decorations 1992.

The Parade, Neath, April, 1974

Familiar faces

A Port Talbot soldier returns home from the First World War to a welcome from his young daughter, 1918.

Elders of Carmel Chapel, Port Talbot, 1918.

Members and officers of Briton Ferry Urban District Council, November 8, 1922.

John and Alice Thomas of Neath with their children, early 1900s. The family owned and ran a bottling business off Windsor Road. They were claimed to be the biggest family of bottlers in Great Britain.

A family gathers outside the door of their home in Heol Y Graig, Cwmavon, 1940.

The members of Crynant butter making class, November, 1929.

These two residents of Dock Street, Aberavon had good reason to smile — they had just heard the news that the Second World War had ended in Europe, 1945.

Two of the residents of Gored Terrace, Melincourt, Resolven, smartly dressed for a special occasion, August 1933.

A family on the doorstep of their house in Victoria Terrace — now Station Road — Pontrhydyfen, late 1940s.

A gathering of the Morgan family from Melyncrythan, 1945.

Committee members of Port Talbot British Legion receive a civic welcome from the Mayor, Alderman Tom Rees, to the town's municipal buildings on a visit there, 1970.

Mary Morgan was the bride at this Neath wedding in 1945.

Officers and committee of Neath Busmen's Welfare Club and Sports Institute, 1944. Eddie Bailey, top right, was the first driver for the N&C Luxury Coach company.

Staff of the Port Talbot goods office of British Railways at a function at the Walnut Tree Hotel, early 1950s.

Members of Elim Four Square Church, Briton Ferry, 1949.

Members of Margam United Football Club at a social evening at Margam Community Centre, December 1954.

Staff of Port Talbot bookmakers H F Shirley enjoy an evening out, early 1960s.

A nursing sister and patient at Cimla hospital, Neath, with a hand made crown, orb and sceptre made to celebrate the Coronation of Queen Elizabeth II, 1953.

Neath-born actor William Squire with members of his family outside the home of his sister in the town's Florence Street, early 1950s.

Officers and committee members of Port Talbot British Legion Club and Branch, 1971.

Three young women enjoy an evening out at Port Talbot Labour Club, 1969.

A group of residents of Wellfield Avenue, Neath, alongside one of the huts near the town's abbatoir, early 1950s.

Guests at a New Year's Eve dance organised by members of Neath Amateur Operatic Society, 1955.

Members of the general committee of Port Talbot Motor Club, 1970.

A gathering of Neath Sunday school children at Wesley Church, London Road, mid-1950s.

This sandcastle building competition at Aberavon Beach was judged by the Mayor of Afan, Councillor Sylvan Thomas, 1976.

Members of the sewing class at Herbert Road Chapel, Melyncrythan, Neath, 1956.

Staff at Neath General Hospital's Glyn Garfield maternity unit, at a Christmas function, 1970.

A charity pram race along Aberavon seafront, June 1979.

A group of Neath Round Table members, mid-1970s.

The Bishop of Llandaff, clergy and choristers at All Saints Church, Cwmavon, shortly before its demolition in 1980.

Special days

Mayor of Neath, Alderman Leslie Morris, with Prince Charles on his visit to Neath during a tour of Wales following his investiture as Prince of Wales, July 1969.

West Glamorgan County Guide Commisioner Miss Freda Gibbins and Neath and District Guide leaders welcome Mrs Olave Baden Powell, Chief Guide, centre, at the opening of the new Neath Guide headquarters, Old Market Street, 1962.

Port Talbot members of the Fish Fryers Association with their families at an annual get together, mid-1920s.

Senior staff, nurses and guests including Ramsay MacDonald, at Port Talbot General Hospital fete, 1924.

Neath Metal Box employees at a presentation ceremony to mark 25 years service 1964.

Civic guests at the official opening of Sandfields library, Morrison Road, Port Talbot, November 18, 1961. The standing figure addressing the gathering is Port Talbot teacher and historian A. Leslie Evans.

Popular Pontrhydyfen singing personality Ivor Emmanuel at Alderman Davies School, Neath, early 1970s.

Musician Winnie Richards Thomas after being presented with a candelabra by members of Neath Methodist Church for 50 years in the church, 1970s.

A presentation evening for a number of men retiring from their jobs as locomotive drivers with the Margam works of the British Steel Corporation, mid-1970s.

A wedding party pictured outside a house in Lingfield Avenue, Sandfields, Port Talbot, 1968.

A retirement presentation evening for staff of the United Welsh Bus Company at Neath Central Club, 1975.

Mayor of Port Talbot May Charles with civic officials and representatives of local organisations at the November 1969 Armistice service at Memorial Park, Taibach.

A trade exhibition staged at the Afan Lido Sports Centre, Port Talbot, 1966.

Deputy Mayor of Neath, Councillor Emlyn Emmanuel, attended this retirement ceremony to mark the retirement of Thomas Arthur Thomas as chairman of Neath Borough Council's unions group, May 1973.

Princess Margaret on a visit to the Llewellyn Alms Houses, Gnoll Park Road, Neath, 1970s .

A retirement gathering for blast furnace gas plant personnel at the British Steel Corporation's Port Talbot steel plant late 1970s.

Out of town

The pier at Aberavon Beach, in some state of disrepair and minus the toll house ticket booth that had once stood at its shoreline entrance, late 1930s.

Giants Grave, Briton Ferry, early 1900s.

A funeral cortege advances across the footbridge crossing the River Ffrydwyllt near Dyffryn locomotive yards, Taibach, Port Talbot, early 1920s.

A Brigade of Yeomanry camp at Margam Park, 1906.

Neath Road, Briton Ferry, 1908.

The now-demolished Jersey Beach Hotel, Aberavon Beach, with sand dunes behind, early 1900s. This picture was taken before the building was severely damaged by fire in 1908.

A view eastwards towards Port Talbot from Ladies Walk, Briton Ferry, 1920s.

The view up the River Neath from Warren Hill, Briton Ferry, showing, from the left: Kennel Row, Llansawel Church and Vernon House, 1930s.

High Street, and Arnold's Corner, Cwmavon, 1910.

Efail Fach, Pontrhydyfen, with the Colliers Arms on the right hand side, mid-1930s.

Looking up the valley towards the viaduct at Pontrhydyfen, early 1920s. Victoria Terrace overlooks the scene.

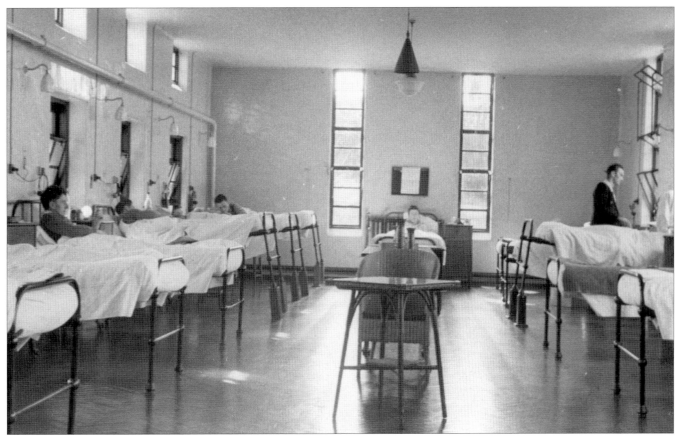

Inside one of the wards at Cimla Hospital, Neath, early 1950s.

The mill at Goytre, Port Talbot, 1920.

Hengwrt Primary School, with Neath locomotive sheds behind, 1966.

Victoria Terrace, Pontrhydyfen, now Station Terrace, 1940. The viaduct can be seen to the right. The lady seated was one of the street's oldest inhabitants.

Peace is the message of this statue at Memorial Park, Taibach, late 1950s.

Construction of local authority homes at Hawthorn Avenue, Baglan early 1950s.

Local authority homes at Bwlch Road, Cimla, Neath, 1981.

Neath Abbey has never been too far away from the march of transport progress as this 1972 panorama shows. First came the Tennant canal, which cuts almost through the centre of the picture, then the railway line from Jersey Marine to Neath below and, when this scene was captured construction work was underway on the A465 Aberdulais to Llandarcy dual carriageway.

Pantyrheol, Briton Ferry, looking eastwards, opposite Neath General Hospital, mid-1980s.

Looking across Cwmavon railway station towards the police station with industrial spoil tips behind, mid-1950s. The tips have long gone and been replaced by housing.

Flood prevention and riverbank strengthening work underway at Velindre, Port Talbot, mid-1980s.

Church
Crescent,
Baglan with St
Catharine's
Church in the
background,
early 1950's.

Looking across the River Neath towards the Ferry Boat Inn, Earlswood, late 1920s.

This South Wales Transport double decker bus came to grief while making a sharp turn off Old Road, Baglan, Port Talbot, before rejoining the nearby A48 in 1958. At the time it was en-route for Margam. It toppled through roadside barriers and ended up on the back kitchens of a number of houses at terraced Ty'r Halen cottages. Fortunately no one was seriously injured and the vehicle was eventually recovered.

Residents of Brynau Wood, Cimla, Neath, use grit to help clear the heavy snowfall of 1982. The field in the background has since been swallowed up by housing development.

Huxtable's garage, on the A48 at Baglan, 1958. The Baglan dual carriageway passes this spot now.

Demolition creeps ever closer for the old Kinema, Hunter Street, Briton Ferry. It had for many years been home to Briton Ferry Little Theatre until shortly before this picture was taken in the mid-1970's.

The high level road bridge at Cymmer, built in 1926, pictured being crossed by a Leyland National service bus in the late 1980s.

Parties and processions

These three young members of the congregation of Neath Wesley Church, were taking part in a Whitsun procession along London Road, Neath, when this early 1920s picture was taken.

When this youngster took part in a Port Talbot carnival in 1934 her message was clear for all.

Will Evans as Lady Godiva in one of Dock Street, Port Talbot's carnival entries, late 1930s.

The second prize winners in Briton Ferry carnival, 1912. Their sign reads: Weary Willie and Tired Tim's first visit to this town.

This horse drawn float pictured outside the Harp Hotel, Neath Road, Briton Ferry, must have drawn plenty of attention during the town's 1912 carnival.

Members of the Queen Mary Stewards jazz band on the march through Cwmavon, late 1930s.

A Whitsun procession at Lodge Cross, Briton Ferry, early 1900s.

James Street, Port Talbot, celebrates the return of two soldier residents after the Dunkirk evacuation of 1940. They were Stan Scourfield, left, and George Wood, right.

Fancy dress time during Festival of Britain celebrations at Church Place, Cwmavon, 1951.

Chapelgoers gather before the start of the Whitsun procession through the streets of Neath, 1910.

Festival of Britain celebrations at Church Place, Cwmavon, 1951.

Children from Farm Road, Briton Ferry, with the chairman of Briton Ferry Urban District Council and his wife during Coronation celebrations for King George VI, 1937.

Port Talbot's Avon Paraders jazz band major, Bill Lang, 1950.

Smartly dressed young members of Siloh Chapel, Melyncrythan, Neath, hold their banner high before a Whitsun march, late 1940s.

Residents of Cove Road and Vivian Park Drive, Sandfields, Port Talbot, tuck into their street tea party goodies during celebrations to mark the Coronation of Queen Elizabeth II, June, 1953.

Employees of the Briton Ferry & Neath Co-operative Society at their annual dinner, early 1950s.

Children from Cove Road and Vivian Park Drive, Sandfields, Port Talbot. in fancy dress during celebrations to mark the Coronation of Queen Elizabeth II, June 1953.

A children's christmas party at Port Talbot British Legion Club, Talbot Road, December, 1956.

Young members of the congregation of Maria Street Chapel, Neath, passing Peglers grocery, Phil Howells butchery and Fred Rist's motorcycle shop in Windsor Road, as they take part in a Whitsun procession, 1948.

One of the floats in the Briton Ferry carnival held as part of celebrations to mark the Coronation of Queen Elizabeth II, June 1953.

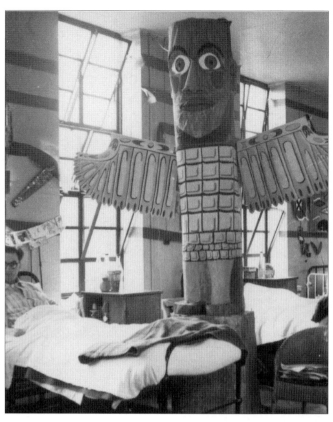

One of the more unusual get well messengers at Cimla Hospital, Neath, early 1950s.

This youngster was enjoying proceedings at a street party in Velindre, Port Talbot, to mark the investiture of the Prince of Wales, July 1969.

Hi jinks at a Port Talbot Naval Club Carnival during the mid-1970s.

Sandfields Sandpipers jazz band lead the Cwmavon carnival procession in the late 1970s.

A social gathering of members of Briton Ferry Townswomens' Guild early 1960s.

Nurses and staff at Cimla Hospital, Neath, during a Christmas party held there during the mid-1960s.

Some of the staff of Woolworths store, Station Road, Port Talbot, at a retirement function, 1970s.

New Year's Eve celebrations at the Jersey Beach Hotel, Aberavon Beach, 1990.

Residents of Bwlch Road, Cimla, during celebrations to mark the investiture of the Prince of Wales, 1969.

Staff of Marks & Spencer's Green Street, Neath, store on the float they entered in Neath carnival, 1984. There was a period theme to the float which reflected the company's origins.

Neath Golf Club members and their partners at their annual dinner and dance, 1982.

Shopping around

Peter Curnow's greengrocery shop at 78 Jersey Road, Blaengwynfi in the Afan Valley. Peter was born in Penzance and came to the area in 1867 and this picture was taken in 1924. The site was later occupied by the Royal British Legion Club. Pictured, from left are: Peter Curnow, shop owner; Henry John Williams, son in law and Winifred Beatrice Williams, daughter.

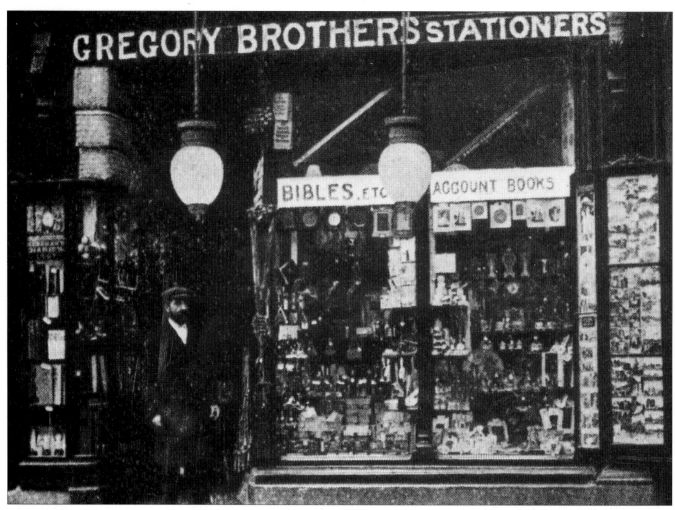

Gregory Brothers' stationery store, 12 New Street, Neath, 1905.

Town centre redevelopment at Port Talbot meant temporary relocation for a number of stores. Among them
L. Longman's butchery and Derrick's record shop which traded for some time at Church Street, late 1960s.

Les Mathias behind the counter of the shop he ran for many years on the corner of New Street, Aberavon. Les retired in 1967 and is pictured above outside the popular premises with his wife Maggie. They began running the shop during the Second World War.

Neath Co-operative store, Windsor Road, mid-1960s — before it suffered the first of two devastating fires.

Shops and the entrance to the Odeon Cinema, in Forge Road, Port Talbot, 1978. By then the cinema had shown its last film and was up for sale. It later became the Majestic bingo club, having reverted to its original name.

Wind Street, Neath, 1970, with Allins the grocers on the left. Boots the Chemist's store now occupies this site.

The new Tesco store in Water Street, Neath, on its first day of opening, September 1978. It replaced an early store in Queen Street.

Ken Richards in his Cambrian Dairies store, Cambrian Street, Port Talbot, shortly before it closed in 1983.

A poultry stall at Neath Market, Christmas 1983.

Station Road, Port Talbot, 1985.

Margaret Gammond's greengrocery shop near Bethany Square, Station Road, Port Talbot, November 1987.

Michael Betts and Graham Rees, two traders at Neath market, 1988.

Allin's the grocers shop at the junction of Water Street and Wind Street, Neath, June 1977 shortly before its demolition.

A wet shopping day in Station Road, Port Talbot, 1986.

Tots
and
teens

Twins Jean and Mary Whiteman with their mum
shopping in Windsor Road, Neath, early 1950s.

Three youngsters dressed as cowboys in Sandfields Road, Aberavon, 1949.

This young girl, a mere 14 months old, was the winner in the baby competition — out of 300 entrants — at Port Talbot Hospital fete and carnival, 1934.

A group of tots in the back garden of a house in Brookdale Street, Neath, 1954.

A young Port Talbot lad out shopping with his mum, 1952.

Bryncoch, Neath, Guides outside the village's Cottage Homes, 1933.

Three teenage girls at Sandfields, Port Talbot, 1953.

Members of the 1st Bryncoch, Neath, Guide troop peeling vegetables for lunch during their 1959 camp at Tenby.

This little Port Talbot youngster looks as though she has found an escape route from her garden, early 1950s.

Three Lingfield Avenue, Sandfields, Port Talbot, boys and their canine chum Rusty, 1957.

A group of Port Talbot schoolboys at a summer camp in Ogmore-by-sea, 1959.

Mayor of Neath, Aneurin Rees, presents cycling proficiency certificates, to young local riders 1963.

Winning smiles from members of the Urdd group at Ysgol Cymraeg Pontrhydyfen after the local eisteddfod, 1983.

Four Corpus Christi participants from St Joseph's School, Pendrill Street, Neath, mid-1960s.

A big moment for this little girl as she makes a presentation to Mayoress of Neath, Mrs Nancy Hemming, watched by her husband, Mayor Gerald Hemming, 1972.

Dillwyn Haines presenting a cake to Kerry Hopkins on receiving her Queen's Guide award. She was the first girl in Cimla, Neath, to receive the award, 1970.

Studious moments in the junior section of Port Talbot's central library, Taibach, 1966.

Cimla Brownies on a summer camp at Bryn Road Guide headquarters, Swansea, 1971.

Two Neath youngsters enjoy a day out at Neath's September Fair, 1973.

Members of the 5th Neath Brownies make a presentation to the Childrens' Ward at Neath General Hospital Penrhiwtyn, 1974.

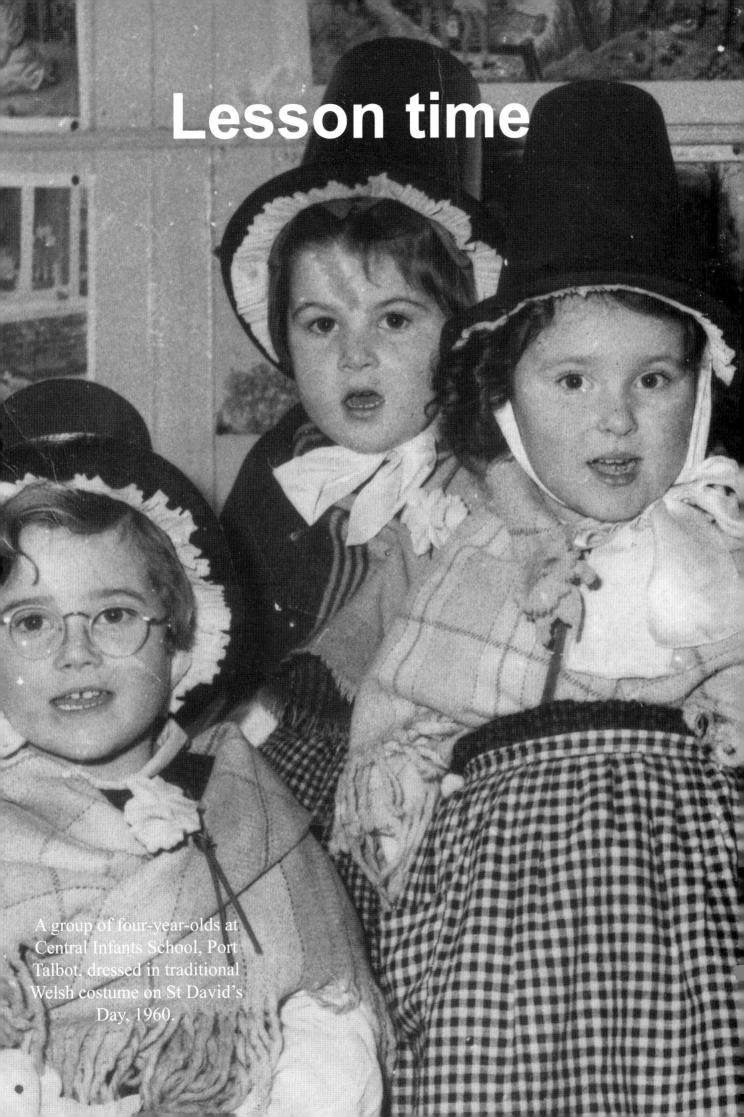

Lesson time

A group of four-year-olds at Central Infants School, Port Talbot, dressed in traditional Welsh costume on St David's Day, 1960.

These children attended the National Board School, Briton Ferry, now the site of the Church of Our Lady of the Assumption, early 1900s.

Standard 6, Central Girls School, Port Talbot, 1920.

Standard 4, Cwrt Sart Girls School, Briton Ferry, 1925.

Class two, Central Girls School,
Port Talbot 1920.

Pupils at Creunant School, in the Dulais Valley, 1909.

Standard 3, Melin Girls School, Neath, 1930.

Class 2, Vernon Place Infants School, Briton Ferry, 1929.

Pupils of Standard III at Eastern Secondary School, Margam Road, Taibach, Port Talbot, 1921.

Some of the students and lecturers at Neath Technical School, 1944-45.

Pupils at the National Board School, Old Road, Baglan, 1920.

Llangatwg Junior School, Cadoxton, Neath, with head teacher Mr Bowen, back left, 1946.

One of the classes of children who attended Cwmavon junior school, mid-1950s.

A class at Blaen Baglan school, Port Talbot, 1970.

Pupils of Tirmorfa junior school, Sandfields, Port Talbot, 1958.

A class at Cwmavon School, 1972.

A class of boys at Alderman Davies Church in Wales School, Neath, 1956.

A class at Traethmelyn Infants School, Sandfields, Port Talbot, 1972.

Form 2C, Neath Grammar School 1953.

Pupils of Cimla Infants School, Cimla, Neath, Wednesday, June 25, 1961.

Pupils of Traethmelyn Primary School, Sandfields, Port Talbot, during an Easter bonnet parade in the early 1970s.

Mayor of the Borough of Afan, Councillor Sylvan Thomas, plants a tree at Bryn Primary School, watched by some of the pupils and head teacher Gerrard Lewis, 1976.

Tonna Infants school pupils enjoy their Christmas party, topped off by a visit from Santa, 1967.

Form 1A Cwrt Sart Secondary School, Briton Ferry, 1968.

Members of the chess team at Central Junior School, Port Talbot, 1978.

A class of pupils at Blaenhonddan Primary School, Bryncoch, Neath, pictured with their teacher, 1960.

Standard 5, Crynallt Infants School, Cimla, Neath, 1971.

Pupils of Baglan Infants School, on St David's Day, 1982.

Form 6A2 Glanafan Comprehensive School, Port Talbot, 1979-80. Also pictured are Headmaster, I R Davies and form master Tom Davies.

Cefn Saeson Comprehensive, Cimla, Neath, gets a new school bus, 1976.

A recorder group at Sandfields Junior School, Port Talbot, 1982.

Some of those who attended Alderman Davies Church in Wales School, Neath, 1978.

Class 5, Central Junior School, Port Talbot, 1980.

Pupils at Hengwrt Primary School, Briton Ferry, 1978.

Members of the percussion group at Herbert Road School, Melyncrythan, Neath, 1968 — under the baton of their junior conductor.

St David's Day celebrations at Bryn Primary School, Port Talbot, late 1970s.

Pupils of Traethmelyn School, Sandfields, Port Talbot, after receiving special presentation spoons to mark the Silver Jubilee of Queen Elizabeth II, July 1977.

Hard at work

These three giant cooling towers were a landmark at BP Llandarcy, Neath, for decades. They were demolished in 1988.

Briton Ferry Ironworks, 1896.

Margam Urban District Council Fire Brigade 1909 under the command of Captain Tom Hughes.

Three terrier bitches pictured with their handler at Baglan. He was possibly a kennel man for one of the big houses in the area, 1920s.

Two employees of the Great Western Railway in the Neath area, around 1910.

Brunel Dock, Briton Ferry, complete with sailing vessels, looking inland, 1910.

Now this Cwmavon vista, from Ynysygwas, is filled with housing, but in 1896 it was a hive of industry.

A Whitford tinplate works gang, Briton Ferry, 1920s.

Skewen Home Guard's First Aid Section during the Second World War, mid-1940s.

Two drivers and two conductors of the United Welsh Bus Company at Neath take a break from their labours, 1950.

Some of the employees of Port Talbot 'Top' steelworks, 1930s.

A group of electrical engineers involved in the instalation of a turbine at a Port Talbot steelworks, mid-1930s.

Construction work underway on the new Melyn plant of the Baglan Engineering Company, ready to accommodate its move from Baglan in May 1953. This view shows the steel skeleton of what was to become the machine shop and also the renovation of the former rolling mill building which was to be used as a welding and fabricating shop before the building of the foundry and melting cupolas.

A group of nurses at Cimla Hospital, Neath, early 1950s.

Four men and a pyramid of ladders — just to paint one of Port Talbot's electric lamp standards, 1939.

Staff at Boots the chemist, Wind Street, Neath, store, 1957.

Tor-Y-Mynydd Colliery, Cwmavon, late 1940s.

Billy Williams and Eddie Beddow, the first members of Neath's Brynhyfryd Bowls Club's Monday gang, early 1960s. This was a voluntary team which helped to maintain the greens.

The Calor Gas Depot at Aberdulais, Neath, 1966.

Usherettes from the Majestic cinema, Forge Road, Port Talbot, 1940. It later became the Odeon and finally until its demolition the Majestic bingo club.

Lorrymen at the Steel Company of Wales, Margam, Port Talbot, early 1950s.

Supervisory assistants at Cefn Saeson Comprehensive School, Cimla, Neath, 1974.

Staff at Sandfields Primary School, Port Talbot, 1955.

The levelled sand dunes at Baglan Bay await the construction of BP Chemicals and the similar chemical production plants that were developed alongside, 1960.

Entertaining ways

PWLLYGLAW.

The drum major and mace bearer of Pwllyglaw Pierrots jazz band, Cwmavon, Port Talbot, mid-1950s.

Port Talbot and District Workmens' Prize Band assemble for a photograph in the back garden of Ty Mawr, Talbot Square, in front of the town's workingmen's club, 1920.

Briton Ferry Independent Labour Party choir, 1937.

Members of Neath Accordion Band, with some of their instruments 1930.

The Aberavon Masqueraders jazz band, with a succession of trophies from a successful season, 1920.

Alfredo's Dance Band, Port Talbot, late 1940s.

Members of Heol Undeb Masqueraders Jazz Band, Cwmavon, early 1950s.

On stage at the New Hall, Aberavon, 1948, are some of the dancer's who formed Trixie Reed's popular and talented dance troupe.

Saxophonists from the successful Ambassadors band, Neath mid-1950s.

The Ambassadors band, Neath, in action during the mid-1950s.

Cwmavon Secondary Modern School Choir, 1953. The choir master was Mr Kinsey.

A Girls Guildery Christmas play at the town's Neath Methodist Church, 1952.

The Christmas pantomime at Llangatwg School, Cadoxton, Neath, 1953.

Port Talbot YMCA Players rehearse for a 1956 production.

Cast of the Neath YMCA's Gnoll Players' production of Bless This House by E. Eynon Evans pictured with group officials and backstage members at the Gwyn Hall, October 9, 1954.

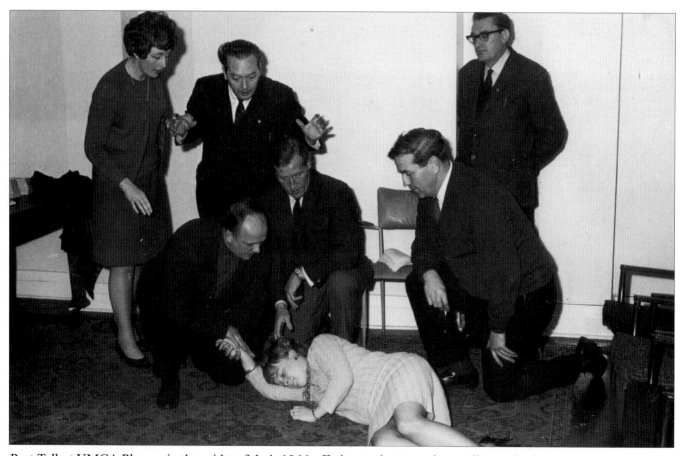

Port Talbot YMCA Players in the midst of their 1966 offering to theatre going audiences in the town.

Some of the young participants in a show at the Afan Lido, Port Talbot, 1980.

Members of the chorus of Neath Amateur Operatic Society's production of Mame, 1976.

Pupils of Bryn Primary School, Port Talbot, who entertained parents and guests at a concert, early 1980s.

Melyncrythan Amateur Operatic Society male chorus members 1983.

Briton Ferry Amateur Operatic Society dancers in its production of Guys and Dolls at the Gwyn Hall, Neath 1994.

Pupils of Dyffryn Comprehensive School, Port Talbot, during a 1980s production of the musical Oklahoma.

Members of the cast of Neath Little Theatre's production of the Wilmslow Boy, 1979. The title part was played by Christopher Waring-Davies, left.

A party of Roman legionaires who took part in a 1980s pageant at Margam Park, Port Talbot.

On the move

A convict ship at Briton Ferry dock, 1905.

This vessel, the Earl of Rosebury sunk off the coast near Briton Ferry. She had left the River Neath loaded with iron but broke her back and sank as the inset picture shows. The incident occurred in 1904.

The Port Talbot Railway & Dock Company's line near its town centre terminus, at Port Talbot Central station, 1900. This was behind the site of today's Plaza Cinema.

One of Port Talbot's early pilot boats — The Briton — at the entrance to Port Talbot docks in the mouth of the River Afan. It was originally an early steam tug boat but was converted to serve as a pilot boat. Abraham crofts, one of the first Port Talbot pilots is seen in front of the bridge, early 1920s.

Just the last few sections to drop into place and the gap is bridged — a view from the Earlswood side of Neath River Bridge under construction, 1953.

A United Welsh Bus Company Bristol RE single deck service bus heads past the Cimla Hotel towards Neath, mid-1960s. It's eventual destination was Swansea.

This Albion bus was operated from Abbey Road, Port Talbot, for many years by local milkman David Walters. The vehicle's registration number was BX 9255. It is pictured in the early 1930s.

David Walters with his milk cart at Port Talbot, late 1920s.

Neath Riverside signal box on the Vale of Neath Railway line 1965.

Dismantling an accident damaged N&C luxury coach — TWN 557 — for spares, 1968. The vehicle was involved in a serious collision in Cardiff that year as the inset shows.

A trio of N&C luxury coaches at the company's Briton Ferry depot shortly before it closed in 1970.

The Marion Byass, the Port Talbot Docks pilot boat that preceded the Margam Abbey, seen on trials before delivery to the port in the early 1940s. During the Second World War it was fitted with a gun emplacement on the bows.

The Marion Byass, the Port Talbot Docks pilot boat seen at her berth in the docks, early 1950s.

The last tradesman's horse and cart in regular use in Neath, alongside St David's Church in the summer of 1972.

Ore from overseas arrives aboard the vessel Gledooch at Margam wharf which was alongside Nos 1, 2 & 3 blast furnaces of the steel Company of Wales Port Talbot works, 1957.

Off for a jaunt on their shiny new Norton 99 motorcycle are these two young riders from Gordon Crescent, Sandfields, Port Talbot, 1959.

Gillard's Garage, Bridge Street, Neath, shortly before the nearby river bridge was closed to traffic, April 1974.

This early bulldozer was constructed from the bottom end chassis of a Second World War Vickers Armstrong tank. Towing its scraper trailer, it was used to level sand dunes on Aberavon seafront to allow for the building of post-war housing and the promenade.

It only just stopped in time! This was the MV Michel Swenden aground in front of the Jersey Beach Hotel, Aberavon, in February, 1957. It was later refloated.

Days out

Local swimmers thronged the lower pond — complete with
its changing huts and diving stage — on the Gnoll Estate,
Neath, in the 1930s as this summertime scene shows.

Crowds throng Aberavon Beach and seafront near the Jersey Beach Hotel on a summer's afternoon, 1920s.

Some of those who enjoyed the Great Western Railway's Neath Mutual Improvement Class annual outing, 1928.

A group of Neath people set off on a charabanc outing aboard an open-topped Dennis vehicle in the early 1920s.

Aberavon Beach, with its the old pier and breakwater, 1910.

A Neath family snapped during an outing to Porthcawl, 1935.

A group of Velindre, Port Talbot, youngsters during a day out in the 1940s.

A family enjoys a paddle at Baglan Beach early 1920s.

Many of those in this group were shop owners or confectioners from Neath who joined a trip to the Somerdale, Bristol factory of chocolate makers J S Fry in 1937.

Residents of Wellfield Avenue, Neath, on an outing to Swansea Beach, 1947. Every year they would collect for a street fund to pay for such a trip.

Three Neath women have their photograph taken with a monkey while sat on a bench in The Square during the town's historic September fair, 1956.

A donkey ride on the beach was always a popular holiday pastime as this Port Talbot girl proved, 1950.

A day on the beach at Aberavon, 1950-style.

All of the staff from Chidzoys fruit and vegetable merchants at stores in Neath and Port Talbot with Mr Wally Chidzoy, his wife, daughter and mother in the centre, 1955.

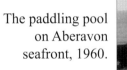

The paddling pool on Aberavon seafront, 1960.

Longford Ladies Club on a summer outing, late 1950s.

Members of the Girls Guildery at Neath Methodist Church, Stockham's Corner, wait on Neath railway station for the train that carried them to their summer camp at Barry, 1952.

The show goes on at Aberavon seafront during a wet summer's afternoon in the early 1960s.

Donkey rides on Aberavon Beach, were a firm favourite in the early 1960s.

Members of Neath ladies Coop Guild on a mid-1950s outing.

Members of Neath Darby & Joan Club prepare to set off on a Gower cruise aboard a paddle steamer 1956. The jaunt was organised by the town's WRVS group.

Members of Bryn, Port Talbot, senior citizens group on a trip to Southsea, 1968.

Staff from Boots the Chemist, Wind St, Neath, outside St. David's Church, viewing a friends wedding, 1958.

Pub crawl

The Castle Hotel, Water Street, Port Talbot, 1925.

The interior of the smoke room of the Castle Hotel, Water Street, Port Talbot, 1925.

The Oxford Arms, Windsor Road, Neath, July 1976 .

The Plume of Feathers, Water Street, Neath, 1959.

The Narrow Gauge Inn, Water Street, Neath, 1972.

The Ancient Briton, Wind Street, Neath April 1973.

The St Ives Inn, Old Market Street, Neath, November 1974.

Port Talbot Progressive Club, also known as the Band Club, 1970.

The Railway Tavern, Water Street, Port Talbot, 1971.

The Bird in Hand , Wind Street, Neath, November 1974.

The Angel Hotel, New Street, Neath, early 1970s.

The Globe Hotel, High Street, Aberavon, late 1960s.

The Red Lion Hotel, High Street, Aberavon, early 1970s.

The Blue Bell and Full Moon pubs, The Parade, Neath, June 1974.

The Avon Vale Hotel, High Street, Aberavon, early 1970s.

Staff behind the highly polished bar of the Avon Vale Hotel, High Street, Aberavon, mid-1930s.

The Full Moon, The Parade, Neath, summer 1975.

The Lamb and Flag Inn, Aberavon, early 1970s.

The Prince of Wales Hotel, Water Street, Aberavon, early 1970s.

The Victoria, The Green, Neath, July 1976.

The White Hart, alongside James Street and The Latt, Neath, March, 1973.

The Jersey Beach Hotel, Aberavon Beach, 1985.

The Apple Tree Inn, Elias Street, Neath, July 1976.

The Three Cranes, Wind Street, Neath, June 1977.

Playing the game

Briton Ferry cycling group, 1898. The trophies suggest success in some kind of sporting event.

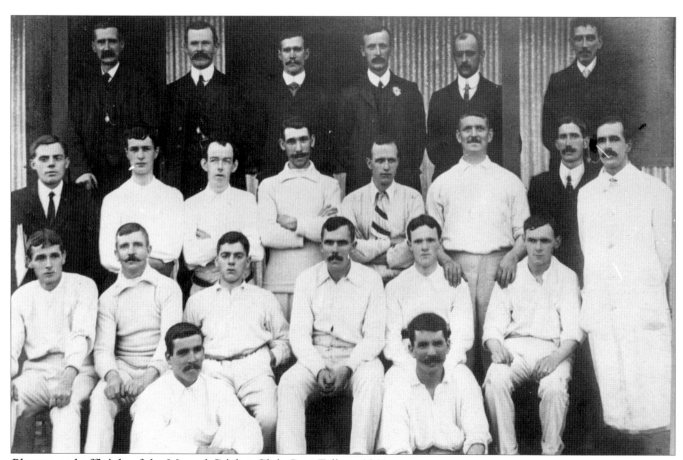

Players and officials of the Mansel Cricket Club, Port Talbot, 1911.

Aberavon Harlequins RFC, Port Talbot League Champions, 1922-23 season.

A cricket match at the Briton Ferry Steelworks ground, 1910.

Baglan Church AFC, were Port Talbot and District Soccer league shield winners 1938-39.

Gnoll Foresters football team, Cimla, Neath, 1949.

Melyn Dynamos football team, Neath, undefeated champions in season 1946-47.

Trefelin School rugby team, Port Talbot, 1949-1950 season.

Rhos Cricket Team, early 1950s.

The last rugby game played on Vivian Park playing fields, Sandfields, Port Talbot, early 1950s. After this match it was soccer only for the ground.

Some of those, including trophy winners who attended the first annual dinner of Port Talbot Soccer League, 1955.

Metal Box RFC at Cefn Saeson pavilion, Cimla, Neath, early 1950s.

Byron Lee being presented with a ring after winning his Welsh schools rugby cap, 1957. Neighbours made a collection and had a party for him. Below: Byron in action at Cardiff Arms Park tackling a Birmingham wing. His efforts paid off for Wales won by 12pts - 3.

Gnoll Junior School rugby XV, Neath, 1955.

Members of Port Talbot Fencing Club pictured receiving bronze coaching awards, late 1960s. Pictured left is Lyndon Martin who later went on to become one of Wales's international fencers. In the centre Dr Norman Spiers receives his award from Wynford Seymour.

This was the first team picture of Metal Box RFC, Neath, after it reformed in the 1962-63 season.

Central Junior School rugby team, Port Talbot, 1974.

One of the rugby teams fielded by Sandfields Comprehensive School, Port Talbot, 1970-71.

Childrens Day at BP Llandarcy, 1972.

Members of Taibach RFC, Port Talbot, mid-1970s.

The Dunes FC, Sandfields, Port Talbot, 1975-76. Winners of the Port Talbot league and cup double they are pictured with club officials.

Metal Box rugby team, Neath, on tour, 1964.

Roger Gale, of Neath, left, and Robert Price, of Swansea who were BP Rally Champions in 1972.

The Amazon women's darts team, Sandfields, Port Talbot, local pub champions, 1978.

The successful Metal Box rugby team which became Neath and District champions in 1973-74 seen with team officials.

Cefn Saeson Comprehensive School, Cimla, Neath, Badminton team 1979.

The rugby squads at Traethmelyn Junior School, Sandfields, Port Talbot, 1976-77.

Briton Ferry RFC, mid-1970s.

A football team at Traethmelyn School, Sandfields, Port Talbot, 1977.

Neath Town Bowls Club, Division One winners 1978.

Neath Boys Club soccer team, 1979.

Port Talbot Naval Club women's darts team, RNA league winners, proudly display their trophies, July 14, 1978.

Cwmavon Junior School rugby XV, 1980.

Glanafan Comprehensive School senior tennis team, Port Talbot, 1980-81.

Cefn Saeson Comprehensive School Cricket team, Cimla, Neath, with the spoils of a very successful season, during the early 1980s.

Some of the working members of Brynhyfryd Bowls Club, Neath pictured during an encounter with the club's retired members, 1980. Unusual head gear seems to have been the order of the day.

A junior rugby team at Traethmelyn Primary School, Sandfields, Port Talbot, 1982.

The football team of Crynallt Junior School, Cimla, Neath, at the end of its successful 1981-82 season.